The Path to the Sea

Other selected titles by the author

A Still Life (The Jargon Society, North Carolina 1977)
Madder Lake (Coach House Press, Toronto 1981)
The Tempers of Hazard (Palladin, London 1993)
Tormentil & Bleached Bones (Polygon, Edinburgh 1993)
One Hundred Scottish Places (October, Eindhoven 1999)
Distance & Proximity (Pocketbooks, Edinburgh 2001)

The Path to the Sea
THOMAS A CLARK

2005

Published by Arc Publications
Nanholme Mill, Shaw Wood Road
Todmorden OL14 6DA, UK

Copyright © Thomas A Clark 2005
Design by Tony Ward
Printed by Antony Rowe Ltd
Eastbourne, E. Sussex, UK

ISBN 1 904614 22 1

Thanks are due to Bob and Susan Arnold's
Longhouse Press for the first publication
of 'Green'; to Peter Riley for bringing out
'Creag Liath' as one of the Poetical Histo-
ries; to Alec Finlay and Morning Star Press
for 'Turning'. Other poems appeared as
pamphlets from Moschatel Press.

Cover photograph by Laurie Clark

The Publishers acknowledge financial
assistance from ACE Yorkshire

Editor for UK / Ireland: Jo Shapcott

CONTENTS

on a clear day
unfasten the gate
and take the path
over the machair
through the orchids
down to the sea

FOREST WITHOUT TREES

to the north the land hardens
it meets and challenges the eye
sandstone, gneiss, quartzite
windswept and empty

a desert of wide skies
rock and water, a sparse cover
of purple moor grass, deer sedge
the light-loving dwarf juniper

rock cascades or stands
eroded by light
in a motionless pouring
insistent and remote

birch, pine and rowan
huddle in ravines
a stonechat drops
its note among stones

the distances are lonely
silence is immediate
immediately lonely
the rough bounds are desolate

you flinch away from it
yet each drop of rain
on your face or your arm
is a point of return

wind combs the heather
it puts an edge on stone
you splash through melt water
shaking the bog cotton

that you may not only
see but feel
the wind pushes against you
abrupt silences fill

settlement is on the edge
of this emptiness
survival is accepting
the wind's caress

the harled dwellings
sit facing the shore
a gentleness of sheep-bitten turf
comes to the door

rusting cars and machinery
rhyme with crottle on the rocks
strewn about in the moment
in a reek of peat smoke

bright talk after winter darkness
is not more welcome
than a lull in the wind
coming home to your own form

time no longer matters
buttercup and ox-eye daisy
iris, foxglove, clover
sweeten the tang of the sea

the seal in the cold water
rises to a clarity
or curiosity, a lapping
of silver, a lapping of grey

mountain line and shoreline
carry the melody
butterwort and milkwort
invite you to delay

a lochan in a dark corrie
a sandpiper's lonely piping
they give their distances
into your keeping

AT LOCH GRINNEABHAT

sandpiper piping from a stone
lifting and lighting
on the same stone
piping on alone

lighting and lifting
out over the loch
in a turn or sally
a swift sortie

small mechanical toy
prompted by a signal
remote from itself
to circle round itself

walks or runs on ground
　　wades in water
will perch on low objects
　　bobbing head and tail

constantly bobbing head and tail
　　flight note a shrill wee twee
by hill lochs by sea lochs
　　sporadically by lowland waters

flies low over water
　　shrill call and flickering wings
a display for no one
　　note heard by stone

will preach from low objects
  turning and returning
to the same theme
  in the half-light in the same tone

a few variations
  on an original air
strong agogic accents
  elaborate grace notes

its pipe is its throat
  the little music
stopped with gammarids
  worms and larvae

dark along the peat haggs
  behind bog cotton
a bleary chink of light
  flickering and throbbing

within the visual field
  you do not occur
lost or taken up with
  what happens to be there

out over a waste
  of dusk again it tries
its circuit brief
  as ripple or dapple

RILLS AND TUSSOCKS

behind cloud
a mountain's
implied weight

rock burned hands
cooled in a
waterfall

a stonechat
chip chipping
at silence

the warm scent
of a strand
of snagged wool

birch saplings
  rising through
  pouring rain

thin birch branch
  more lichen
    than birch branch

after rain
  wind shaking
    light from trees

a glow for
  one moment
  on a stone

washing with
raindrops from
pine branches

the blast from
a gust of
goldfinches

cool smooth wet
black pebble
half submerged

a terse note
repeated
farther in

an empty
ochre-brown
ice-scoured land

yellow flags
tall beside
a green lake

nine paces
leading to
nine places

odd little
water song
lost again

came the nine joys
with the nine waves
with the nine joys
of the nine waves
and the nine waves
of the nine joys

the first wave to meet you
the second wave to lift you
the third wave to balance you
the fourth wave to carry you
the fifth wave to farther you
the sixth wave to enjoy
the seventh wave to rock you
the eighth wave to prepare you
the ninth wave to deliver you

CREAG LIATH

island of many inlets
shape bitten by tides
little bays in which to linger
spray reaching to its shoulder

a few strides east to west
out of kilter south to north
island of peaks and corries
remote, bright, various

its obscurity lifting into clarity
a lonely place to be alone
sunbeams sharpened on its ridges
acid water in rock pools

it is a place apart, grey
a thin wedge in blue
where you were left abandoned
by an impulse or a tide

island persisting in itself
drawing the mist about it
firm ground to stand on
in a tilting sea and sky

with hills implied behind cloud
soil impoverished by rain
a few sheep pull at a thin
crop of sedge and drawmoss

island exposed and sheltered
fertile of colours and forms
contained place in which to be
both accurate and expansive

ruined dwellings on open moors
wild goat paths through heather
paths with nowhere to go
where there is nothing to do

among the sedimentary deposits
intrusions of coarse-grained granite
with crystals of amethyst, topaz
blue-beryl, smoky quartz

having rare flowers in profusion
by burns, in flushes, on wet rocks
strewn across meadows, solitary
in crevices, on ridges and crags

with remnants of woodland
birch, rowan and aspen
huddled in ravines
gullies of fern and bracken

a quiet to drive out sense
a wind to lean against
a wind that can drop
to make you doubt your shape

to the east bare and tranquil
shifting dunes to the west
some couch grass to stabilise
peat sweetened with blown sand

sandpiper piping from a stone
lifting and settling on a stone
far cry of a curlew
a corncrake clearing its throat

the hours long and inconsequential
waving glumes of marram grass
the days harsh and tender
primroses in a nest of rock

where strict limits engage
particulars, set at a distance
from distraction and noise
balanced on the crest of a wave

every distance has an internal duplicate
which can be measured and sustained

a glimpse of the sea in a fold of hills

the distance recedes in exact proportion
as things draw near

the weight of a stone in the palm of your hand

under the twists of water
among the pondweed

the slender naiad

among the duckweed
under the braids of water

calm was expected
but not this clear space
of blue between clouds
rare as a latin inscription
above the door of the ruin
of a black house

THE HIGH PATH

let's take the high path
that clings to the cliff edge
    through the ripe barley
past the corn marigolds
taking up this and that
    dropping this or that

like a rag or a flag
    space flaps in the wind
fluttering and settling
    between scabious
    and knapweed the sea
flutters lightly away

trust the tangled path
the sea at your elbow
  it will lead you through
complex information
meadow-grass and bent-grass
  to a fine sea view

in among the grasses
  are the manifold
spaces little places
  where intention is
  no longer gathered
but ramified dispersed

pale comfrey flowers
linger in green spaces
in the tall bracken
as if such places were
formed by bracken for
pale comfrey flowers

melancholy thistle
rest harrow, milk vetch
climb through the long grasses
to add at random
a touch of colour
to the drift of colours

the waves are dancing
and the light bounces back
　into a larger
atmosphere or climate
that you move in gladly
　in receipt of light

over the tall grasses
　the blue sky stretches
an unimpeded blue
　you can lie back in
　crushed grasses and let
your head fill up with blue

swallows swooping low
over the ripe barley
respond as keenly
to the intelligence
as barley to the least
rumour of a breeze

barley combed by the wind
ripples with warm light
as if the light were not
given but contained
given out when combed
by the light-seeking wind

the waves of barley
the ripples of the sea
    flow in or out from
your feet as you pass through
the ripples of barley
    the waves of the sea

as a hawthorn will show
    the prevailing wind
in a motionless gust
    of whipped-back branches
    you take the shape of
what you know let it go

THE SHAPE CHANGER

once I was a deer
stepping under trees
my form always broken
by lights and shadows

then I was a wildcat
leaping up and away
from the traces of my own
rigour and ferocity

in a fold of hills
nodding with flowers
I took on many
shapes and colours

seldom was I present
to myself in a form
half as alluring
as what I might become

again I was a goldcrest
a bright fragment of song
moving through the forest
leading farther in

at times defeated
reduced to stone
I lay disregarded
concealed in the open

then I was a juniper
turning to take the slope
pausing and bracing myself
above a sheer drop

and once I was a dragonfly
for an afternoon
little more than a notion
of the stillness and the green

GREEN

the dark hills
lie darker
on water

the colours
nourished by
recent rain

reflected
green ripples
on beech boles

showers of
light shaken
from willows

light sprinkled
about in
bracken glades

now here and
now there in
bracken glades

a stillness
littered with
stripped spruce cones

green fold that
will open
out again

something slips
away from
inspection

little pulse
in the air
dying out

for the breeze
a delay
of birch leaves

a grey trace
turning in
the drenched grass

AT DUSK & AT DAWN

before the day begins
or when the business of the day
is over there are intervals
densities of blue or grey
when you stand on the brink
of a different possibility
a stillness that opens
out into clarity or
a subtlety that folds
back into stillness again
you might almost touch it
an occasion in the air
as steady as a great tree
branching into delicate life

to sit out in the air
and take the shape of the air
its cool spaciousness and precision
and never mind what comes to mind
but attend and cease to attend
remaining cool and spacious
this is the poise of being alone
to be one and no other
and at the same time discover
your shape as a mere integument
that is less a shape than a notion
let it blow away or drop
sitting on a bench in the garden
as the sun goes down or comes up

clinging to willow leaves
clinging to grasses, the mist
disperses and reassembles
alternately masking and revealing
shifting opacities in the dusk
the mist is an insistence
the more tenacious because
it does not insist but gives way
before every advance towards it
closing in again around
whatever ground has been gained
there is no ground to be gained
the clinging mist and the dusk
have erased every advantage

as it sets or rises, the sun
throws light against the canopy
of leaves that spread to contain
its force and to infuse a green
light or glow through the wood
the air has a grain of light
which is almost tangible
but is so evenly distributed
it nowhere waits upon a surface
or sharpens to confuse a form
the space is of light and air
high, neutral, undisturbed
by bird song or by the fire
held behind the screen of leaves

the shadow extends the tree
from substance to possibility
where the tree stands, it walks
while the tree talks, it is silent
it is not a part of the tree
it is not apart from the tree
it comes and goes with the sun
and offers shelter from the sun
the tree is focused in its shadow
at each moment it is at rest
though each moment may be its last
at dawn the shadow is released
and at dusk it will again become
closer to the tree than its name

in the half-light of dusk
after the day has prepared
hard surfaces for inspection
before the night has plunged
things back into themselves
there is a settlement in which
the external and the internal are
continuous with the evening air
if you are alone at the edge
of shadows you are not alone
the hours of light shine in you
with a compacted energy that
also burns in tree and stone
partly revealed and partly veiled

sit for a while on a stone
on the slope above the river
relax and let the light drain
back to the dense tree shadows
before long someone will come
and sit with you on the stone
not beside you but taking up
exactly the space you occupy
it is the one you left behind
on every journey out of yourself
transparent, weighing nothing
breathing with you when you breathe
come to take up residence again
to look out through your eyes

walk for a while beside a river
and beneath the sound of flowing water
or within the sound of flowing water
you will begin to hear and feel
that which does not sound or flow
if you walk alone beside a river
and listen to the sound of rushing water
the haste and the din of rushing water
will stun you into stillness
if you stand for a while beside a river
the little ripples and eddies of water
the whorls and vortices of water
may rob you of the power to move
with any purpose or direction

worked into the texture
of the dusk, into the air
as into a ground, is a reserve
a tone or implication
in which something is withheld
over there where the path
feints in a sepia mist
it flickers, drawn back
briefly into an impatience
of form that is again subsumed
a breath away from emptiness
it is now present with equal
tension throughout a locality
that it gathers from the air

at dawn and at dusk the pools
the little pools are lakes
that ripple out and hold
fractured and reformed images
that drop into a larger dimension
dark cloud and darker tree
confuse with baroque contours
the place where earth meets water
where leaf canopy becomes sky
and one who was passing by
has been detained by distances
that might be heights or depths
earth, water, air or fire
in a break on a stretch of moor

as longing stretches out
and begins to detach itself from
the initial object of longing
it becomes present everywhere
and can be found in everything
forming and informing everything
the weight of this stone is longing
the curve of that tree is longing
and longing makes the lightest breeze
sigh in the tall dead bracken
longing is not for this or that
but is longing for itself alone
to know itself in late afternoon
longing is a kind of lingering

a bird so light it can arrive
the same moment as the morning
weighing little more than a shadow
suddenly on the highest branch
to rest at the top of its impulse
without disturbing a leaf
hardly bending the light
with the plain shape of a leaf
but more detached from the branch
it can drop through the tree
through a play of shadows
and as suddenly rise
without the aid of a breeze
where a leaf can only fall

far out on the headland
there is a graveyard by the sea
where a few carved stones
lean among uncarved stones

the waves play around it
seals come in to enquire
the dead are glad to sleep here
ragwort nodding in the sunlight

the rippling of the waves
the trembling of the leaves

the sparkling of the waves
the glinting of the leaves

the splashing of the waves
the rustling of the leaves

the dancing of the waves
the turning of the leaves

the rushing of the waves
the drifting of the leaves

is it far when you think of it

is it grey when you think of it

is it cold when you think of it

is it clear when you think of it

is it small when you think of it

is it there when you think of it

the far-glimpsed island

the clear-seen island

the mist-veiled island

the wave-rocked island

the spray-washed island

the sun-bathed island

TURNING

on turning to take
the steep hill slope
there is a lightness
where your own shape
and weight are forgotten
in an access of brightness

and though the day is dark
turning brings a clarity
as if a gentle rain
had renewed each possibility
of sea, air and hill
moss, grass and stone

it is a moment only
when the heather and gorse
are clear and strange
and present with the force
of immediate things that will
immediately change

steady yourself
on the curve of the hill
that pushes against you
dig in your heel
and let the sky settle
into place about you

now the wind describes
the curve of your cheek
and now in a lull
of wind there is the ache
of stillness, of sunlight
on primrose and tormentil

in a transition as swift
as from standing to falling
or from awkwardness
to mobility of feeling
one wide arc might link
severity to excess

as you bear down
on the slope you are lifted
above it into sky
and the weight that was shifted
from one foot to another
has fallen away

each gesture is at once
large and precise
so much is at stake
as each gesture is
released from the last
a skua scolds from a rock

at each turning there is
a chance of the recovery
of near and far
to step out of the scenery
of accomplished fact
into a privilege or air

in turning around
you may open up a space
in everything you know
and if you have the grace
and tenacity it may
be somewhere you might go

on a clear day
unfasten the gate
and take the path
over the machair
through the daisies
down to the sea

THOMAS A CLARK was born in Greenock, Scotland.

His poetry has been consistently attentive to form and to the experience of walking in the landscape, returning again and again to the lonely terrain of the Highlands and Islands.

In 1973, with the artist Laurie Clark, he started Moschatel Press. At first a vehicle for small publications by Ian Hamilton Finlay, Cid Corman, Jonathan Williams and others, it soon developed into a means of formal investigation within his own poetry, treating the book as imaginative space, the page as a framing device or as quiet around an image or a phrase, the turning of pages as revelation or delay.

From 1986, Laurie and Thomas A Clark have run Cairn Gallery, one of the earliest of "artist-run spaces", specialising in Land Art, Minimalism and a lyrical or poetic Conceptualism. After many years in the Cotswolds, the Clarks moved in 2002 to re-open the gallery in a small fishing village in Fife in Scotland.

In addition to his books and smaller publications, Clark has also made site-specific installations in galleries, in gardens or in the landscape, and has many works in permanent collections world-wide.